THE EXTRAORDINARY EB-1

The Title Run of Edgar Bolaños

Franky D Gonzalez

BROADWAY PLAY PUBLISHING INC
New York
www.broadwayplaypublishing.com
info@broadwayplaypublishing.com

THE EXTRAORDINARY EB-1
© Copyright 2022 Franky D Gonzalez

Cover image created using DALL-E

First edition: October 2022
I S B N: 978-0-88145-954-8

Book design: Marie Donovan
Page make-up: Adobe InDesign
Typeface: Palatino

THE EXTRAORDINARY EB-1 was developed by
Urbanite Theatre (Summer Dawn Wallace, Brendan
Ragan; Artistic Directors) in Sarasota, Florida, as
part of the 2020 Charles Rowan Beye New Play
Commission.

CHARACTERS

EDGAR BOLAÑOS, *Central/South American. 28. Male*
MAMÃ, *Central/South American. 31. Female*
BOY, *Central/South American. 8. Male. (can be played by an
older actor who can pull off the sense of an 8-year-old)*
ARMANDO GONZALEZ, *Cuban defector. 41. Male*
MANUEL GARCIA, *Latino, US citizen. 32. Male*
REFEREE, *White. U.S. citizen. 53. Male*
COYOTE 1, *can be played by the actor playing* REFEREE
COYOTE 2, *can be played by the actor playing* MANUEL

NOTE ON MUSIC

For performance of copyrighted songs, arrangements or recordings referenced in this play, permission of the copyright owner(s) must be obtained. Other songs, arrangements or recordings may be substituted provided permission from the copyright owner(s) of such songs, arrangements or recordings is obtained, or songs, arrangements or recordings in the public domain may be substituted.

Round 1

(Bare stage. EDGAR BOLAÑOS *stands alone in boxing attire.)*

EDGAR: What they don't tell you about boxing is that when they say it's mostly mental, what they mean is, how well can you stay focused despite getting the wind knocked out of you. What they mean is, how good does your brain work when they get scrambled by some fucker's uppercut.

Boxing's mental. Yes. But the rest is instinct and reaction. You react to his shoulder movements. He steps, you step. It's like a dance of death in the ring. You train to make fighting part of muscle memory. When he throws a punch, you counter. You feint, you cut off the ring. You learn to clinch and fight on the inside, till it's instinct. The greatest boxers had the best reactions.

But we ain't talking about great boxers here.

We're talking about those ones. You know which. They get a fanbase because they got their nation behind them or they're a hometown kid doing their gym proud. We're talking about those kids who didn't have no other option because there's no school and bills needed paying.

We're talking about those men who stare across the ring at the other man, and both of 'em put their bodies on the line so their family don't gotta go to the streets to get paid.

We're talking about guys who fight to get that visa, who throw a hundred punches a round trying to catch a green card in that part of the fist where fingers and palm meet.

We're talking about the fighters who lay it all on the line and fail.

We're talking about the truly American sport.

Where fighting for your kids means denying a dad and his kids their chance at a better life. It's a sport whose champions are made by the one who destroys his opponent. It's the single man on top of the mountain of shattered dreams and broken men.

We're talking about an eight-year-old who gets found in a freight train going to America, and all he's got is some boxing gloves his mom gave him before she died trying to get her son in to this country. So, the coyotes throw you in the ring to pay off the debt for smuggling you in.

We're talking about decision to take out ten men in the ring in one year's time, all to avoid getting deported.

We're talking about sitting in saunas trying to burn weight all to stay in the place you call home.

Because EB-1 visas aren't given to boxers unless they got the belt.

We're talking about…

(EDGAR *collapses to the floor and begins vomiting.*)

Round 2

(*The lights rise on the stage. Freight train compartment, a long wooden bench on the wall of the compartment. Sounds of a train and its horn. As the lights rise the train begins to move. The door to the compartment opens and a* BOY *wearing boxing gloves is tossed in while a* MAMÁ *climbs aboard holding a gun, searching for anyone inside. She slams the compartment door closed.)*

BOY: I don't like this game.

MAMÁ: Me neither.
Let's stop playing and rest.

EDGAR: Who won?

MAMÁ: You did.

BOY: How did I win?

MAMÁ: You got on the train first.

BOY: Why are we here?

MAMÁ: We're going on a vacation.

BOY: This doesn't feel like a vacation

MAMÁ: How would you know?
You've never been on vacation.

BOY: How long do we have to stay here?

MAMÁ: Until we get there.

BOY: Get where?

MAMÁ: Away from here.

BOY: Why do we need to leave?

MAMÁ: It's a vacation.

BOY: Can't we have a vacation in our home?

MAMÁ: Then it's not a vacation.

BOY: Then what is it?

MAMÁ: Unemployment.

BOY: What's that?

MAMÁ: When you stay home all the time.
Because you're not working.

BOY: Do you work on vacations?

MAMÁ: No.

Could you stop asking so many—?

BOY: Will it be nice where we're going?

MAMÁ: It'll be a surprise for both of us.

(Gunfire. The MAMÁ *and* BOY *duck. They slowly raise their heads.)*

BOY: Mamá, I'm scared.

MAMÁ: Me too.

BOY: Why is it so dark in here?

MAMÁ: To help you sleep.

BOY: Why are we in a train?

MAMÁ: You don't like trains?

BOY: I like them. But is this the right one?

MAMÁ: It's all we could afford.

BOY: Why can't we afford to go on a plane?

MAMÁ: Planes are expensive.

BOY: How much is this train ride?

(Sounds of yelling and gunfire as the train moves.)

BOY: Mamá—

MAMÁ: You have to be quiet now.

BOY: But—

MAMÁ: Shut up.

(The BOY *falls silent. The compartment door shakes. The* MAMÁ *aims her gun at the door. It stops shaking. They breathe out a sigh, and she lowers her weapon.)*

BOY: What are we going to do?

MAMÁ: We wait till we get to our vacation spot.

BOY: Was a plane too expensive because of me?

MAMÁ: Yeah.
But that's okay.

BOY: I don't think it is.

MAMÁ: Well, I don't have much choice.
It has to be okay.

BOY: Why don't you have much of a choice?

MAMÁ: It doesn't matter.

BOY: Why doesn't it matter?

MAMÁ: Because when do we actually have a choice in anything?

BOY: I don't know.

MAMÁ: Exactly.

BOY: Mamá...

MAMÁ: Baby, please. I'm tired.

BOY: Sorry.

(The MAMÁ *sighs.)*

MAMÁ: What's up?

BOY: It's hot.

MAMÁ: Yes.

BOY: Do you have water?

(The MAMÁ *gets a bottle of water and tries to give it to the* BOY *who spills it.)*

MAMÁ: Fuck.

BOY: I'm sorry.

MAMÁ: That was our only bottle.

BOY: Please don't be mad.

MAMÁ: Just...
It's okay.

It's gonna be fine.

BOY: You promise you're not mad?

MAMÁ: No, I'm pissed.

BOY: Oh.

MAMÁ: But it's going to be okay.
So, no point in getting mad.
We just have to be careful next time, okay?

(Silence)

BOY: Okay.
(After a moment)
Can you tell me what it's like?

MAMÁ: What?

BOY: Being a mamá. What's it like?

MAMÁ: That's tough to answer.

BOY: Why?

MAMÁ: Because you wouldn't understand.

BOY: Could you tell me anyway?

(Silence)

MAMÁ: I don't know. I guess it's…well. A parent doesn't know what kind of child they're bringing into this world. You gotta wonder, right? If you knew how your kids would turn out, would you have them? Would you think that it's worth it to have a baby if you knew it wasn't going to do much in this life? Or maybe if they die early? Or maybe they turn out absolutely awful? I noticed I asked myself a lot of questions when I got pregnant. The usual suspects.
Will my baby change the world?
Will my baby love me?
Will my baby get rich?

But what I was really asking was, "Will my baby prove that I made the right decision?" Or if we take it further, maybe I was asking, "Will my baby prove that, yes, I am a good person."

These are selfish questions. But they are questions. They are my questions.

And at the end of their lives, I think more than a few parents aren't very happy or, at least, they aren't thrilled with the answer to these questions in their heart of hearts.

This is the stuff we won't confess. And there are more than a few people who would get mad at me right now. They'd say that they would never think such things about their children. But I know the truth.

That anger comes from them feeling like someone's intruded on something personal. Those thoughts, those secrets, that's not for the air to take along the current and whisper into the ears of others. No, those secret thoughts, they are meant only to be between God and the Parent.

Not to say that every baby's bad or something. But c'mon. They're not, you know, "great."

But sometimes you're left wondering, "Did I make the right choice putting everything aside so that another life can have a chance?"

And you wonder if it's worth it.

BOY: Am I worth it?

(Long silence)

BOY: You don't have to tell me right now.

(The BOY and MAMÁ exit.)

Round 3

(Press conference. EDGAR *on one side of a podium while* ARMANDO *sits alone on the other. The* REFEREE *enters and stands at the podium.)*

REFEREE: Fight fans, welcome to our lead-up
To the match between Edgar "The Extraordinary EB-1"
Bolaños
And Armando "El Final" Gonzalez
Gentlemen, thank you for attending.

ARMANDO: My pleasure.

EDGAR: Yeah.

REFEREE: Now, Edgar the oddsmakers
Have you at a 42 to 1 to lose.
People in the industry say
That you're too inexperienced
And that your record is filled
With a list of—

EDGAR: Look, I already know.
This is all I gotta say,
They put those odds at 42 to 1.
That's their business.
But I'm gonna win.
How many times in boxing
We see men get old in the ring?
Armando's past his prime.
I'mma give it to him,
Six years ago, he woulda won.
But this ain't six years ago.
It's now.
Armando is gonna lose now.

REFEREE: Armando
Edgar brings up valid points.

Your distinguished career
Has had you in many grueling fights
Is it possible you've lost too much
At your age in this sport?

ARMANDO: I have no comment about my age.
Regarding my opponent,
I do not underestimate Edgar.
He has fought nine opponents
And knocked each of them out.
Regardless of who he fought
Nine knockouts means he can cause damage.
We will see what differences
Age and experience against
Youth and knockout power have.

EDGAR: You got no comments because
You know the truth.
You gonna get old in that ring
And I'm gonna knock you out.

(ARMANDO *smiles as if to say "We'll see".*)

REFEREE: Armando, there are those who wonder why
you're still fighting
After all your accomplishments as an amateur.

ARMANDO: My family has waited patiently while I
tried to live my dream
Of winning a world title.
I gave up my homeland, my parents,
The love of my people, and time with my children for
a belt.
I have failed twice. I won't fail again.
I take this fight because
Time is no longer on my side.
Edgar is right. I am getting old.
I cannot wait another few years

To work my way up the ladder again.
I gave up everything for this belt.
He has knocked out nine people?
My record has triple the knockouts.
I am willing to risk his punches
To get one more shot.
When we meet in the ring
I will knock you out, Edgar.

EDGAR: Yeah, right.

REFEREE: Powerful words.
Edgar, there have been concerns
About your weight in the past.

EDGAR: Yeah.

REFEREE: In your last two matches
It's been rumored that you
Resorted to dangerous measures—

EDGAR: I do what I gotta do
To get what I need to get.
I'm gonna make weight.
That's all I gotta say.

REFEREE: Is it an option to move up
A weight division?

EDGAR: Absolutely not.

REFEREE: Why's that?

EDGAR: I'm on the verge
Of becoming mandatory for the title.
Moving up in weight right now
Basically means gotta start over.
I worked too hard to start over.

REFEREE: You've been a professional
For about a year now.
There are other boxers who have invested

Time and worked their way up the ranks...

EDGAR: Did they fight nine times in one year?

REFEREE: There are coaches and promoters
Who believe that's dangerous.

EDGAR: It's a sport where your job
Is to hit the motherfucker in front of you.
Jesus Christ, no matter what you do, it's dangerous.

REFEREE: There is speculation that you
Could very well be overexerting himself
From the dangerous weight cutting
And fighting so frequently.

EDGAR: Look, just get to the point
What are you actually trying to say?

REFEREE: You were spotted recently
Leaving an immigration center—

EDGAR: Yes.

REFEREE: It's no secret that your moniker "EB-1"
Is a reference to the visa you're trying to earn.
Do you feel you're rushing into this too soon
To avoid deportation?
You can't deny there's risks taking this many fights—

EDGAR: I'm taking good care of myself.

REFEREE: You and what team?
Sources say that your usual corner quit.
And you've offered half your purse
For coaches to be in your corner
Just so bouts can go forward.

EDGAR: Yes.
I'm rushing into this fight.
And yes, there's a chance
That doing this'll fuck with my health long term.

I didn't ask for this, I don't want to do this.
Most days, I'm tired from all the training.
I get what people are saying.
But this's what I gotta do, and I'm okay with that.
If staying here in the US means fighting for the title
Against a hundred guys tomorrow.
I'mma fight, just like anyone when
When people try to take you from your home.
I'm out of time just like you, Armando.
Difference between you and me?
You left home searching for the world title.
I'm looking for the title so I can stay home.
You fight harder trying to keep your home.
That's why I'm gonna win.

REFEREE: The question remains.
The EB-1 visa is rather well-known.
It provides permanent residency.
If it was something of an option,
Why did you wait until the last minute
To try to get an EB-1 visa?

EDGAR: I didn't know about it.

REFEREE: Really.

EDGAR: This shit's a shakedown.
Fuck this, man. Fuck this.
(He stands up and exits.)

REFEREE: Last question, Armando.
You are a 42 to 1 favorite to win.

ARMANDO: Yes.

REFEREE: Do you think the odds are about correct?

ARMANDO: Wish they were lower.
Make a little more money
Betting on myself to win.

(The REFEREE *laughs.* ARMANDO *mulls on something.)*

Round 4

(Freight train compartment. Dimly lit. The MAMÁ *sits alone, polishing her gun. The* BOY *enters.)*

MAMÁ: Go back to sleep.

BOY: I can't sleep.

MAMÁ: I'm not sleeping so you can get some rest.

BOY: Then you sleep and I stay up.

MAMÁ: That's not how this works.

BOY: How does it work?

MAMÁ: The mother tells her child to do something
And the child does it.

BOY: Why do I have to sleep?

MAMÁ: Because if you don't want to sleep now
You'll want to sleep when I need you to stay awake.

BOY: But I'm not tired.

MAMÁ: I can tell.

BOY: I don't think we're actually on a vacation.

MAMÁ: I knew didn't raise an idiot. Thank God.

BOY: Why are we here?

MAMÁ: Because we are fleeing.

BOY: What does that mean?

MAMÁ: It means running away.

BOY: Why are we running?

MAMÁ: Because we were in danger.

BOY: Why did you say it was a vacation?

MAMÁ: Because it was easier to tell a lie than the truth.

BOY: Why did you lie?

MAMÁ: Because sometimes a lie is the fastest way
To shut people up.

BOY: You mean you lied so I'd be quiet?

MAMÁ: If I tell the truth will you be quiet?

BOY: Why do people lie?

MAMÁ: Why do you lie?

BOY: I don't lie.

MAMÁ: Really?

BOY: Okay, maybe I lie sometimes.

MAMÁ: Why?

BOY: That's why I asked you.

MAMÁ: I gave you my answer.
Lying got you to shut up.

BOY: Where's papi?

MAMÁ: Why are you asking that question?

BOY: I want to know.

MAMÁ: You already know the answer.

BOY: You said he was getting better
After he got hurt.

MAMÁ: You believed me?

BOY: You said he was getting better.
That he'd catch up with us.

MAMÁ: I need you to learn a lesson.
Never believe anyone
Who tries to convince you
That you didn't see what you saw.

BOY: So, you lied again.
Does everyone lie?

(Silence)

MAMÁ: Honestly, yes.
I think everyone does lie.

BOY: I want to go home.
Right now.

MAMÁ: We are going home.

BOY: This train is taking us back?

MAMÁ: No. We have a new home.

BOY: Where?

MAMÁ: North.

BOY: You bought us a new home?

MAMÁ: No, but we'll get one.

BOY: Do they give away houses in the north?

MAMÁ: You have to buy it.

BOY: With what money?

MAMÁ: I'll get it.

BOY: How?

MAMÁ: By getting a job.

BOY: What job?

MAMÁ: Won't know until we get there.

BOY: Why can't we go back to our old home?

MAMÁ: Because we were in danger.

BOY: What's danger?

MAMÁ: It means not safe.

BOY: Why is home not safe?

MAMÁ: Because it wasn't a home anymore.

BOY: Why not?

MAMÁ: Because when a house becomes a grave

It can never be a home again.

BOY: Papi's dead.

MAMÁ: Yes.

BOY: That's why you have his gun.

MAMÁ: Yes.

BOY: Why did you take his gun?

MAMÁ: It's what he left behind.

BOY: That's all?

MAMÁ: It's the only thing men leave behind.
Legacies of violence.

BOY: How did he die?

MAMÁ: Like men do.
Thinking they're more than what they are
Laying down everything for their pride.
Then leaving wives and mothers
To pick up the pieces of glass shattered
By their stupid fucking egos.

(*Silence*)

BOY: I don't understand what you mean.

MAMÁ: Of course you don't. You're a man.

BOY: Explain what you said earlier.

MAMÁ: Can't do it.
I don't even understand my own words.

BOY: Then why are you saying words
If you don't understand them?

MAMÁ: Because I'm stupid.

BOY: No you're not.
You're the smartest.

(*The* MAMÁ *shakes her head and polishes the gun.*)

MAMÁ: Get some sleep.

BOY: I'm scared.

MAMÁ: Me too.

BOY: What are we going to do?

MAMÁ: I don't know yet.

BOY: But there's a home waiting for us?

MAMÁ: Yes. There is.
Now go to sleep.

(Silence. The BOY *makes his way back to the hiding place but stops.)*

BOY: Mami?

MAMÁ: Yes?

BOY: Are you lying?

MAMÁ: Would it matter?

(Silence)

BOY: Mami?

MAMÁ: Last question and you go to sleep.

BOY: When we get to the north.
Can I get a job to help buy our house?

(Silence)

MAMÁ: Sure.

BOY: What kind of job should I get?

MAMÁ: I don't know.

BOY: I'll think of one.

MAMÁ: Think of one later. Now sleep.

BOY: Tell me a story?
Please?

MAMÁ: *(Sighing)* Okay.

(The BOY *rushes to the* MAMÁ *and hugs her tight. She
wraps an arm around him and he stis on her lap. Gun still in
hand.)*

MAMÁ: Once upon a time
Before the age of violence
There was a young—and beautiful—queen
And her kinda cute prince…

BOY: Are you talking about us?

MAMÁ: Wait and see.
Now, these two were going
On a quest to a faraway land.

BOY: Why?

MAMÁ: Because they were in grave danger.
Monsters had already taken away the King
And the Queen, fearing for her son
Took the both of them and dressed like you and me
To take him to a land where they wouldn't…
Where it wouldn't hurt anymore and…and…

BOY: Mami?

(Silence. The MAMÁ *mouths something. The gun slips out of
the* MAMÁ's *hand. The* BOY *stands up.)*

BOY: I'm gonna go sleep now…
*(He goes back toward his hiding place. He looks at the gun
on the floor. He hesitates. He exits.)*

Round 5

(A table, two chairs at center. ARMANDO *and* EDGAR
opposite each other. The REFEREE *stands at the center of the
ring.)*

REFEREE: And now.
For your amusement

For your viewing pleasure.
Twelve rounds of boxing.
For the right to battle champion Manuel Garcia
For his title.
A battle between two immigrants
At the end of their ropes.
The question will be answered today.
Who goes on? Who keeps a dream alive
For one battle longer?
Who says farewell to greatness?
Who stays in the running?
Tonight we'll see the clashing of not two men,
But the clashing of two souls
Putting their lives on the line
For the dreams of a lifetime.
To the audience in attendance.
And to boxing fans all over the world.
Are you ready?

(A deafening silence. ARMANDO *and* EDGAR *face each other.)*

ARMANDO: You look like shit.

EDGAR: Yeah.

ARMANDO: Why?

EDGAR: Cost to play the game.

ARMANDO: You know you can't knock me out.

EDGAR: I gotta try.

ARMANDO: You know you can't beat me over twelve rounds.

EDGAR: Won't know till the final bell.

ARMANDO: It's hopeless.

EDGAR: I'll take those odds.

ARMANDO: You're stupid.

EDGAR: But I'm still here.

ARMANDO: You can't guard yourself for shit.

EDGAR: I can take a punch.

ARMANDO: I been through a lot to get this belt.

(Silence)

EDGAR: I know.

ARMANDO: And I'll never get another chance.

EDGAR: Yes.

ARMANDO: You're not going to win.

EDGAR: You don't know that.

ARMANDO: I'm better than you.

EDGAR: Yes.

ARMANDO: This has been my dream since…

EDGAR: Since I found out they're gonna take me away.
Since you were a kid.
Since the belt's been around everyone's wanted it.
We've had a rough road, man.
I'm not trying to take that from you.
But I'm not gonna lose here.

ARMANDO: I'm gonna knock you out.

EDGAR: You can try old man.

REFEREE: Alright gentlemen.
Good. Clean. Fight.
Nothing below the belt.
Defend yourselves at all times.
Obey my instructions.
Touch gloves.
C'mon, touch 'em.
Alright. God bless.

(A bell rings. ARMANDO *and* EDGAR *assume a fighting stance. They trade punches.)*

ARMANDO: Give up.

EDGAR: No.

ARMANDO: You're gonna die.

EDGAR: Then I die.

(Silence)

ARMANDO: Staying here mean that much to you?

EDGAR: It's all I want.

ARMANDO: Why?

EDGAR: Fuck you.

(Another exchange. ARMANDO *and* EDGAR *freeze.)*

ARMANDO: America don't care about you.

EDGAR: They don't gotta care about me.
But they sure as shit ain't getting rid of me.

ARMANDO: Okay then…
I came to the United States
Seeking a better life for myself.
What a unique story, right?
I made really good money.
I got endorsement deals.
I own two houses
But the world title was always out of reach.
I was always the contender, the gatekeeper.
The third or fourth best. The perennial also-ran.
(Silence)
My dad was old school.
When I defected from Cuba
To him it was like I betrayed the family.
Wouldn't talk to me.
Wouldn't even talk to his grandchildren.

Both times I failed to get that title
I heard my fucking father.
That's how the fucking pigs
Got their propaganda.
Lure some dumbass like me
With promises of championships
And when the dumbass left la isla.
They fuck you.
Maybe it's true…
(Silence)
A you know in your head that most dreams…
Most dreams go nowhere.
It's just that…
You never think that it's your dreams
That are going nowhere.
I don't know…

(Silence. EDGAR *hasn't taken his eyes off* ARMANDO.*)*

ARMANDO: I forgot where I was, but one time
My wife asked me if it was time to hang up the gloves.
I told her I couldn't do it.
I gave up too much to walk away without a belt.
I can't just…
But imagine 42 to 1 odds…
The odds will never be that good again.
(Silence)
All I ever dreamt of was winning a world title.
Ah well. It was a good dream.
At least my children'll never have to punch anyone to
pay the bills.
(He smiles.)
That's worth all the belts in the world.

*(*EDGAR, *goes to* ARMANDO *who opens his arms up for an
embrace. They embrace. After a moment, the embrace turns*

into grappling. They separate. EDGAR *delivers a haymaker right to* ARMANDO's *face.* ARMANDO *falls. A crowd cheers wildly and the* REFEREE *waves off the fight. A bell rings.* EDGAR *holds up his glove in triumph.)*

Round 6

(Freight train compartment. MAMÁ *and* BOY *sit together.)*

BOY: Mami?

MAMÁ: Yes?

BOY: I have a question.

MAMÁ: I hope I have an answer.

BOY: Where do we go when we die?

MAMÁ: To heaven.

BOY: Does everyone go to heaven?

MAMÁ: Only the good people.

BOY: Where do the bad people go?

MAMÁ: Hell.

BOY: What's that like?

MAMÁ: Lots of fire and demons
Hurting you forever.

BOY: That's scary.

MAMÁ: You don't sound scared.

BOY: I'm not a bad person.
Why should I be scared?

MAMÁ: I'm jealous.

BOY: Are you a bad person, mami?

MAMÁ: I don't know.
Sometimes I think I am.

BOY: Why?

MAMÁ: I do bad things sometimes.

BOY: Like what?

MAMÁ: None of your business.

(Silence. The BOY *stares at the* MAMÁ *with those eyes.)*

MAMÁ: I do things like say bad words.

BOY: Ooooh, that's really bad.

MAMÁ: Yep.

BOY: You need to say sorry.

MAMÁ: To who?

BOY: I don't know.

MAMÁ: Well, when you find out, tell me.
I'll say sorry to them directly.

BOY: Do the bad people die?

MAMÁ: Yes. They eventually all go away.

BOY: But not good people.

MAMÁ: No, they die too.

BOY: But the bad guys always die.
Not the good guys.

MAMÁ: Next lesson. Everyone dies.
Good and bad.
Nobody escapes death.

BOY: Not even me?

(Silence)

MAMÁ: You don't have to worry.

BOY: But I'm scared.

MAMÁ: I thought you were a good person.
Whatcha got to be scared of?

BOY: What if there's nothing?

MAMÁ: What?

BOY: What if there's nothing after this?
Or what if I am a bad person
And I don't that I am?
Do people who are bad without knowing
Get treated the same as a person who chooses to be
bad?

MAMÁ: We all think we're doing the right thing.
Nobody knows that they're bad.

BOY: So, are we bad?

MAMÁ: I don't know.

BOY: It's all scary.
I don't want to go to hell when I die.

MAMÁ: You won't.
You're just gonna go to sleep and go to heaven
When you die.

BOY: Will papi be there?

MAMÁ: God, I hope not.

BOY: What?

MAMÁ: I'm sure he's gonna be there.

BOY: Will you be there?

MAMÁ: I think so.

BOY: It's not heaven without you.

MAMÁ: What's heaven look like?

BOY: You and me together.

MAMÁ: Is that all you want in heaven?

BOY: That's all I want.
(Silence)
Are we almost there?

MAMÁ: I think so.

BOY: Where are we now?

MAMÁ: Somewhere in Mexico.

BOY: How much longer?

MAMÁ: Maybe a day.

BOY: How long have we been here?

MAMÁ: Too long.

BOY: I'm thirsty.

MAMÁ: We'll get water soon.

BOY: Can you die
If you don't drink water?

MAMÁ: Yes.

BOY: Am I going to die?

MAMÁ: No.

BOY: How do you know?

MAMÁ: Same way you know you're going to heaven.

BOY: This feels like hell.

MAMÁ: Yes.

BOY: But this will be over soon.

MAMÁ: Yes.

BOY: I got a question.

MAMÁ: You have a lot of those.

BOY: How do you get to heaven?

MAMÁ: Well, we have to die first.

BOY: How do we get there if we're dead?
Our bodies don't move.

MAMÁ: Well…we have souls.
Souls leave the body when we die
And go to heaven or hell.

BOY: But where is heaven?
And where's hell?

MAMÁ: One time I was told
That black holes lead to other universes.
Maybe souls travel really fast
To a black hole that'll take you to heaven.
And other souls go to a black hole to hell.

BOY: Is that true?

MAMÁ: Or maybe they get trapped
In the emptiness of space.
The endless void.

BOY: Why would they get trapped?

MAMÁ: Maybe all the good things you do
Make your soul lighter and able to take the journey.
But all the bad things you do make your soul too heavy
And they can't make the journey to heaven.

BOY: Wow…
(Silence)
Or maybe something takes the souls there
And if you're good you get a ticket.

MAMÁ: Like what?

BOY: A train?

MAMÁ: A soul train?
Really?
(She laughs.)

BOY: Are we going to heaven right now?

(The MAMÁ's laughter dies.)

MAMÁ: What?

BOY: Is this a train ride to heaven?
Are we already dead?

MAMÁ: Don't talk like that.

We're just going to another country.

BOY: What do other countries have
That ours doesn't?

MAMÁ: Safety.

BOY: But if we're all going to heaven
What do we have to be afraid of?

MAMÁ: The people who killed papi.

BOY: But they're going to hell.

MAMÁ: Yes, but we shouldn't be trying to die
Just because we think we're going to heaven.

BOY: But why be afraid?

MAMÁ: I don't know.
I don't know.

BOY: Unless maybe there's no heaven?
Like I thought.

MAMÁ: There's a heaven.

BOY: So then why are you afraid?

MAMÁ: Because I'm not going to heaven, okay?

BOY: But you're good.

MAMÁ: I'm not.

BOY: Why do you think that?

MAMÁ: I don't want to talk about it.

BOY: Okay.

MAMÁ: Just…can I have a moment alone?
Please?

BOY: Alright.

(The BOY exits. The MAMÁ stares off, far away. The BOY
reenters.)

BOY: Why are there countries?

MAMÁ: I thought I told you I needed a minute alone.

BOY: It's important, mami.

MAMÁ: There are countries because different people
Have different ideas
About how to live their lives.
When a bunch of people agree
On how they want to live together
They make a country.

BOY: Does everyone have a country?

MAMÁ: Everyone is born in one.

BOY: And is that their country?

MAMÁ: Most times.

BOY: So there are times when
People don't have a country?

MAMÁ: Yes

BOY: What happens to them?
Where do they go?

MAMÁ: I guess they look for one.

BOY: Do we have a country?

(Silence)

MAMÁ: No.

BOY: Are we going to find one?

MAMÁ: I hope so.

BOY: But right now we don't have one.

MAMÁ: No.

BOY: Do bad people have countries?

MAMÁ: Not all of them.

BOY: Do good people have countries?

MAMÁ: Most do.

BOY: Does it mean we're bad
If we have no country?

MAMÁ: No. We didn't choose this.
You have to choose to be bad.

BOY: But you said most people don't know that they're
bad.
Are we choosing to be bad?

MAMÁ: No. It doesn't—

BOY: What if you having your own country is heaven?

MAMÁ: What?

BOY: The good place.
Where things are safe and you're okay.
That's what we're looking for.
Is the country we're going to heaven?

MAMÁ: I don't think so.

BOY: I don't want to go to hell!

MAMÁ: You're not going to hell.

BOY: But you said the country—

MAMÁ: It's a good country.
It's just no heaven.

BOY: But it's safe?
And good people are there?

MAMÁ: Yes, there are bad people, too
But mostly it's good.

(Silence. The BOY hugs the MAMÁ.)

BOY: One last question.

MAMÁ: What?

BOY: What happens to the people
Who never find a country?

(Silence)

Round 7

*(*EDGAR *training in a thick sweatsuit. Shadowboxing and jumping jacks.* ARMANDO *enters.)*

EDGAR: Fuck you doing here?

ARMANDO: You trying to lose weight?
(Silence)
You're doing it wrong.

EDGAR: It's worked fine before.

ARMANDO: Getting harder to take off the weight though, right?

EDGAR: Fuck off.

*(*EDGAR *stumbles. Suddenly the stage rumbles and chaotic lights start flashing.* EDGAR *convulses while standing.* ARMANDO *rushes to* EDGAR, *concerned.)*

ARMANDO: Get the fuck out of my way.
Move. Move. That's my fighter.
Champ—champion.
How you doing?

(The lights snap back to normal and the rumbling ends. ARMANDO *separates from* EDGAR.)

EDGAR: *(Steadying himself)* I'm good.

ARMANDO: You look like shit.

EDGAR: Why you asking questions
If you already got the answers?

ARMANDO: You should quit.

EDGAR: You already know
That shit ain't happening.

ARMANDO: You can re-cross the border.

EDGAR: No.

ARMANDO: Why?

EDGAR: Because I don't want to.

ARMANDO: Bullshit.

EDGAR: Believe whatever you...

(EDGAR *collapses.* ARMANDO *goes to him.*)

ARMANDO: C'mon, take that shit off.

(EDGAR *stands up and with* ARMANDO's *help and takes off the sweatsuit.* EDGAR *is clearly dehydrated.*)

EDGAR: Whatcha think?

ARMANDO: Jesus Christ....
Who the fuck taught you how to weight cut?

EDGAR: Self-taught.

ARMANDO: I can tell.

EDGAR: Look, man—

ARMANDO: Let me be your coach.

(*Silence*)

EDGAR: Man, get the fuck out.

ARMANDO: I'm serious.

EDGAR: Why?

ARMANDO: Because I want you to stay
In this country.

EDGAR: Fuck's it matter to you?

ARMANDO: The man who beat me
Had better become the world fucking champ.

EDGAR: So, this is about you.

ARMANDO: Yes.

EDGAR: Why should I accept your help?

ARMANDO: Because Manuel Garcia is a world champ.
He's one of the best pound for pound.
If you don't got an actual coach in your corner
You gonna get killed.

EDGAR: I can't afford to pay a fee.

ARMANDO: I'll do it for free.

EDGAR: That makes no sense.

ARMANDO: It doesn't need to.
You need a coach.
I'm gonna get you a world title and a visa.

(Silence)

Round 8

(Sauna/ Freight train compartment. The BOY *sits next to the* MAMÁ *.* EDGAR *watching.)*

BOY: Mamá?

MAMÁ: Yeah?

BOY: Why did you choose the United States?

MAMÁ: They can help us the best.

BOY: Help us how?

MAMÁ: Help us with starting a new life.

BOY: Do they help everyone that goes to America?

MAMÁ: Yes.

BOY: So, everything will get better?

MAMÁ: When we get there, yes.

BOY: But I don't understand.

MAMÁ: What?

BOY: Why are we hiding?

(Silence)

MAMÁ: What do you mean?

BOY: Why do I have to stay in a hiding place?
Why aren't there chairs on this train?
Why didn't we take a bus?

MAMÁ: It's easier this way.

BOY: Are we doing something wrong?

MAMÁ: We're protecting ourselves.

BOY: From what?

MAMÁ: It's really difficult to explain...

BOY: Why is it difficult?
Are we hiding or not?

(Silence)

MAMÁ: Yes. We are hiding.

BOY: Why?

MAMÁ: Because...

BOY: Are we sneaking into America?

MAMÁ: No.

BOY: Then why are we hiding?

MAMÁ: Because...

BOY: Are we not allowed into America like normal?

MAMÁ: We can go...just...

BOY: Then why do we need to hide?
We just have to say that our old home is dangerous.

MAMÁ: It's not that easy.

BOY: Dad is dead because of how bad it is.

MAMÁ: You need to understand
It's very complicated.

BOY: Help me understand. Explain it.

MAMÁ: They might deny us if we go the normal way.

BOY: Why? We're in trouble.
You said they'd help us.
Why would they deny us?

MAMÁ: I don't know.

BOY: But you know everything.

MAMÁ: But I don't.
I just don't.
You need to understand.
I don't know anything.
I'm just as scared
I don't know what to do.
I just need to make sure you're safe.
I need to make sure you get to the US.

BOY: Why me?

(The train stops abruptly. Yelling outside. Doors opening. A moment later, gunshots and screaming.)

MAMÁ: Get to your hiding place.

BOY: What?

MAMÁ: NOW!!

(BOY and MAMÁ both exit. A rumbling and chaotic lights. EDGAR convulses before falling to the ground. A few moments later ARMANDO enters and rushes to EDGAR.)

ARMANDO: No, no, no.
Get up. Come on now.

EDGAR: I'm not…I'm not gonna…

ARMANDO: You're not going on me now.

EDGAR: *(Groggy incoherent)* I'm the one…go on the train for my soul.

ARMANDO: That's right, that's right.
Whatever you say, Eddie.
No, don't, don't fall asleep.

EDGAR: I can't breathe.

ARMANDO: We gonna get you to a hospital.

(ARMANDO *helps* EDGAR *to a bench. The lights snap back to normal. The rumbling stops.*)

EDGAR: I don't need water, Coach.
I need to sweat more.

ARMANDO: You got no more sweat in you.

EDGAR: Then I gotta find more sweat.

ARMANDO: I'm getting you out of here.
C'mon, get up.
I said get up.

(EDGAR *struggles up and stumbles into* ARMANDO *who catches him.*)

ARMANDO: How long you been in the sauna?

EDGAR: Few hours.

ARMANDO: I fucking told you to do it in intervals.

EDGAR: Lose more faster if I stay here longer.

ARMANDO: That's not how that fucking works.

EDGAR: You didn't explain it good.

ARMANDO: No, you're just a stubborn asshole.

EDGAR: You're a shitty coach.

ARMANDO: Can't help being shitty.
My boxer's a shit student.

EDGAR: Good enough to kick your ass.

ARMANDO: Funny.

EDGAR: Nah. Truth.

Let's check my weight.

ARMANDO: No, we need to call off the fight.

EDGAR: What we need to do
Is get my ass on the scale.

(EDGAR *forces himself to the scale and steps on.* ARMANDO *looks down.*)

ARMANDO: You're still six pounds over, Eddie.

EDGAR: Fuck.

(EDGAR *gets off the scale and starts jogging in place.* ARMANDO *stops him.*)

ARMANDO: No.

EDGAR: I gotta make weight…

ARMANDO: No.
First we talk.

EDGAR: We don't got time to talk…

ARMANDO: We do.

(ARMANDO *takes hold of* EDGAR *gently and guides him to the bench.*)

ARMANDO: Eddie, man…
We can postpone the fight.

EDGAR: We can't.

ARMANDO: Then we need to talk.

(EDGAR *gets up and jogs in place.*)

ARMANDO: Sit the fuck down.

(EDGAR *stops. He sits.*)

ARMANDO: We're gonna talk for a bit.

EDGAR: Okay.

ARMANDO: I only got one knockout in the first round to my name.

I don't believe in brawling.
Brawling is how you get fucked up.
Boxing is about hitting and not getting hit.
But a few years back I was facing this guy.
Rodgers was his name.
If I beat him, I get to be mandatory for the belt.
So, I wasn't gonna risk shit, you know?
Get the decision or wear him down until he gave up.
Didn't matter to me, as long as I won.
Plus, Rodgers was tough as fuck.
Nobody you wanted to get into a war with.

EDGAR: Get to the fucking point, Armando.

ARMANDO: But this guy came up to me
A few days before the fight with an offer.
If I got a knockout in the first round.
He'd record and take pictures
And get it to my family.

EDGAR: Why the first round?

ARMANDO: The odds of me getting a knockout
In the first round was like 21 to 1.
I wasn't known as a knockout artist.
My own team wouldn't take that bet.
But I told him to take out as many loans
And get all his money together.
I was gonna get that knockout.

EDGAR: Did you?

ARMANDO: Yeah, but Rodgers fought hard.
Broke my hand and had a concussion.
But I got him good, left hook to the chin.
My family got to see me again.
And that guy made a shit ton…

EDGAR: So, what's this story about?

ARMANDO: Nobody risks their life
Just because they want something bad.

EDGAR: Okay…

ARMANDO: So, then?

EDGAR: What?

ARMANDO: Who you doing this for?
You tell me that, and I'll get that weight off you.

*(Silence. EDGAR stares at ARMANDO. The BOY and MAMÁ
re-enter. They stare at EDGAR who sees them. A low rumble.
EDGAR looks ready to fall. ARMANDO follows EDGAR's
stare.)*

ARMANDO: Eddie…

EDGAR: I don't need a fucking backstory
To prove I deserve to stay in this country.

(Silence)

EDGAR: My mother died to get me here.
I get kicked out then it feels like I failed her.
Okay?

ARMANDO: Okay.
C'mon.

*(ARMANDO and EDGAR exit. The MAMÁ pushes the BOY
away, but he goes right back to her.)*

MAMÁ: You need to go hide now.

*(The BOY senses what's to come. He hugs the MAMÁ .
The yelling increases in volume and rattling from the
compartment doors grows more violent.)*

MAMÁ: To answer your question…
Every moment. Every heartbeat
From your first breath to my last gasp.
This very moment.
Worth it.

You're worth it.

EDGAR: Why?

MAMÁ: Because you're extraordinary.

(With a very gentle nudge from the MAMÁ *, the* BOY *goes to hide. She approaches the compartment door. She draws her weapon. The door opens in a flash of powerful light. She leaps out firing her gun. A scuffle, shots fired. Silence. The compartment door shuts. He comes out holding his boxing gloves close. The train starts to go.)*

Round 9

(Bare stage. A table and three chairs. EDGAR *and* MANUEL *on opposite sides. The* REFEREE *sits upstage of the two boxers.* ARMANDO *is standing by* EDGAR *giving last minute tips.)*

ARMANDO: These press conferences
Are an opportunity and a trap.
They try to psych you out
Get in your brain and make you lose
Before you even throw a punch.

EDGAR: Okay, Mando.

ARMANDO: Whatever trick he pulls.
Don't fall for it.
Let him insult you
Let him insult me.
Just get through this interview
Intimidate him with what we practiced.

EDGAR: I know, Coach.

MANUEL: C'mon, Armando.
You can't protect him forever.

(ARMANDO *leaves* EDGAR *and stands off to the side,*
watching closely.)

REFEREE: Thank you both for taking this interview.

EDGAR: Yeah.

MANUEL: Whatever, man.

REFEREE: Manuel, let's start with you.
You've been quite vocal
About your desire to fight Edgar.
Could you speak more to that?

MANUEL: I don't like him.
I don't like what he does.
I see him I wanna tear his head off.

REFEREE: What about Edgar causes these emotions?

MANUEL: What are you fucking kidding me?
The disrespect, the fucking nerve of this guy.
Thinking that boxing's his easy way into staying in this
country.
Fuck you, man.

REFEREE: Would you say you have an anti-immigrant
bias?

MANUEL: Fuck outta here with that PC bullshit.

REFEREE: That's not answering the question.

MANUEL: And fuck you right the fuck back.

REFEREE: Is there any reason that you're facing Edgar?

MANUEL: Edgar's the mandatory.

EDGAR: They had to force you to face me.

MANUEL: Fuck you say?

EDGAR: You wouldn't take me on
Till it was required.

MANUEL: Keep talking.

EDGAR: I'm just getting started.

REFEREE: Edgar, this match means much more to you
Than just a title and becoming champion.

EDGAR: Yeah.

REFEREE: For a long time
You've been calling yourself
The Extraordinary EB-1
That's the name of the visa
That you're applying for.
Could you talk a little about that?

EDGAR: Yeah, man. I mean
It's the extraordinary visa.
I'm an extraordinary boxer.
I'm the Extraordinary EB-1.

(MANUEL *snorts and shakes his head.*)

REFEREE: To qualify for that visa outright
You need to win a distinction
That acknowledges you
As one of the best in your field.
In boxing there is no higher distinction
Than a world title.

EDGAR: That's right.

REFEREE: Why did you choose boxing?
Of all sports?

EDGAR: I'm good at hitting and getting hit.

REFEREE: Yes, but...

EDGAR: It is what it is.

REFEREE: How did you come to this country?

EDGAR: I was little.
Like seven or eight.
My mom got me out.

My dad was already dead or something.

REFEREE: Where is your mother?

EDGAR: She died on the way up.

REFEREE: To the US.

EDGAR: Yeah.

REFEREE: How did you survive?
A child in the US.
Not knowing the language.
Not having anyone.

EDGAR: You either survive or die, man.
I chose not to die.
Became a boxer.

REFEREE: And this match
It's just another means
For survival.

EDGAR: That's all it's about.

REFEREE: Manuel.
Hearing that…
What are your thoughts?

MANUEL: What thoughts?

REFEREE: About Edgar?

MANUEL: About the motherfucker
I'm gonna help deport?

EDGAR: You need to win
Before you talk about deporting me.

MANUEL: You think we need to get in the ring
For me to send your ass back?

EDGAR: You ain't shit.

MANUEL: You're soft, kid.

EDGAR: We'll see.

MANUEL: Three rounds.
That's all I give you.
Round 1 to remind you
Where the fuck you belong.
Round 2 so you give up
And start learning the Spanish you forgot.
Round 3 to knock you the fuck back
To your ratshit country.

EDGAR: That mind game shit
Don't work on me, hermano.

MANUEL: Mind games?
You think the shit I say
Are fucking mind games?
Nah, homie.
Mind games is thinking
That hard work and beating has-beens
Is gonna let you stay here.
Mind games is thinking this country wants you.
Mind games is thinking
You're extraordinary.

EDGAR: Fuck outta here.
I proved myself.

MANUEL: Fuck you talking about?
Oh shit. Oh wait.
You think you knocked him out?
You actually believe—
Oh shit. Oh shit. Oh shit.
You don't know?
He threw that fight.

REFEREE: Are you implying that Armando—

MANUEL: What you think this immigrant fuck
Actually knocked out Armando Gonzalez
And that shit wasn't rigged?

Don't matter how old you get.
You don't get caught by a punch that wide
Unless you're getting paid to take that hit.

EDGAR: Fuck you.

MANUEL: Oh, you thought your shit was legit.
You didn't know?
Ask Armando, ask him right now.

ARMANDO: Don't listen to him, Eddie.

EDGAR: What's he talking about?

ARMANDO: He's fucking with your head.
Don't fall for that shit.

MANUEL: You want fucking with your head?
Here's fucking with your head.
You need this belt to get your visa.
Maybe I should vacate this title.
Right now. Right the fuck now.

REFEREE: Are you implying
That you're going to vacate your title
So that he can't win it in a fight?

MANUEL: I think that's exactly what the fuck I should do.
I told you. I fucking told you.
We don't need to fight
For me to send you the fuck back.

ARMANDO: Fuck you, man.
You wouldn't do that.

MANUEL: Fuck I need the belt for?
People pay to see me
Not this trinket.
I save money if I get rid of the belt.

REFEREE: Are you vacating the title?

Right now, are you vacating?

ARMANDO: *(Voice rising)* Don't do Eddie like that,
Manuel.

Don't you fucking dare.

MANUEL: And what if I fucking do?

ARMANDO: *(Overlapping)*
Eddie has worked too hard
For you to take his chance from him
He did everything they told him
He ran himself ragged trying
To get this fucking visa
And you will not, you will not,
You will not fucking do this to my boy.
He played by the rules
He never said no.
He fought till he was almost dead
He never complained, not once.
He deserves to stay in this country
He's earned it
This country's his home.
Why is it, why is it always shits like you
That try to take someone's dream?
He loves this country
Even when it tries to fuck him over.
Give him his fucking shot.
Don't steal this from him.
You fucking piece of shit.
You can't do this to him, you can't do this
You can't do this, you can't do this.
You can't fucking do this to Eddie.
He's earned this, he's fucking earned—
You motherfucking paper champ.
You'll never be shit 'cause your coward ass

Won't take a fight like a man.
You ain't no champion, you fucking clown
Call off the fight. Go for it. If my boy
Gets his ass deported then everyone'll know
That you're a fucking coward that won't—
Eddie'll take your head off—
Belt or not, he'll win
But you ain't taking what's he's earned.
Fuck you, man. Fuck you.
You wanna bring up the past
This shit ain't about—
Oh yeah? Then motherfucking—
FUCK YOU!!

MANUEL *(Overlapping)*
I don't have to give this kid shit.
This isn't some fucking pity party bullshit.
He can try and try and try and fucking try
But if he don't get shit from this life
Then that's what he deserves.
Because he does not fucking matter.
How many fucking people did me and him
Knock out getting here?
How many people's dreams we crush?
How many people deserved a shot
But ain't getting that chance because this—
This fucking bullshit immigrant fuck took
That chance from people who gave
Everything to the sport.
Using boxing as a fast way to get a visa.
Fuck that.
I ain't stealing shit from him
This belt ain't his to decide how it goes
I'm the fucking A-side here.
I decide if this fight's for a belt or not.

I'm the fucking immigration.
I'm the United fucking States of America
And if I want to reject his fucking plans
Then I will reject them, no explanation.
So you and your fuckass two-bit
Amateur shit kid can go right the fuck back
To where he came from.
I own the belt, I am the champion.
If I want to call off the fucking fight
And delay it till his ass is deported
Then I'll fucking do that.
Keep that shit talk up old man.
Your boy wanna fight me like a man
Do it without a belt on the line.
Do it for the honor and not a fucking visa
Fuckass fake coach.
Using this immigrant shit to live a dream.
When you couldn't get a belt yourself.
No matter how hard you fucking tried
Because you wasn't shit back in the day.

(ARMANDO *rushes to* MANUEL *and lobs a haymaker
that* MANUEL *dodges. The* REFEREE *gets in between the*
ARMANDO *and* MANUEL. EDGAR *stays seated, unable to
move. The lights begin flashing and the rumbling sound
returns.*)

REFEREE: Stop. Stop. Stop.

MANUEL: Look at that.
Can't even hit me
While I'm sitting.
Shit fucking boxer.
Shit fucking coach.

ARMANDO: Fucker
Fuck you.

Fuck you.

Fuck—

(EDGAR *falls to the floor in convulsions.*)

REFEREE: Subdural hematoma.

MANUEL: We'll have to remove a portion of skull.
Prevent the swelling

ARMANDO: On what side's the hemorrhage?
That's where we'll shave.

REFEREE: Jesus, what the fuck happened to him?

ARMANDO: Boxing match.

MANUEL: What's fucked up is he just won a world title.

REFEREE: Ah, the poor brown fucker.

(*All except* EDGAR *exit, who remains on the floor, though no longer convulsing.*)

Round 10

(*Freight train compartment/sauna. Sounds of a train and its horn. As the lights rise the train begins to move. The* BOY *sits alone, still wearing his boxing gloves.* EDGAR *sits up and looks around before spotting the* BOY. *The* BOY *waves.* EDGAR *is surprised.*)

BOY: Hi.

EDGAR: Hey.

BOY: Got any water?

EDGAR: Sorry…

BOY: Of course not.
Who are you?

EDGAR: I'm…

BOY: Are you a boxer?

EDGAR: Yeah.

BOY: Are you really good?

EDGAR: I think so.
I'm fighting for the world title tomorrow.

BOY: Do you have a nickname?

EDGAR: The Extraordinary EB-1.

BOY: What's that?
EB-1?

EDGAR: Well, it's my initials.
Edgar Bolaños Number 1.
Get it?

BOY: I think so.

EDGAR: It's also the name of the visa I wanna get.

BOY: Visa?

EDGAR: Permission to stay in the United States.

BOY: Oh.
You're not American?

EDGAR: Nah.
Why? Did you think I was?

BOY: Yeah.
You look American.

EDGAR: What's American look like?

BOY: Like you.

EDGAR: You're funny.

BOY: No, I'm a boy.
Why do you need permission to stay?

EDGAR: What?

BOY: In America. Why do you need permission?

EDGAR: I came in without permission

A long time ago.
America found out.
They said I gotta go back
Or I can get this visa
For being an extraordinary boxer.
That's why I'm trying to get the EB-1 visa.

BOY: That's not what I'm asking.

EDGAR: Sorry, I guess I don't understand your
question.

BOY: You took too many hits to the head.

EDGAR: You a comedian?

BOY: No. Just thirsty.
You speak Spanish?

EDGAR: Used to.
Lost it all.
How you speak English so good?

BOY: You don't speak it too well now.

EDGAR: Yo, I'm trying to be nice.

BOY: I speak English
Because you need me to talk English.
I'm gonna need one of those visas, too.

EDGAR: Why?

BOY: Who taught you how to box?

EDGAR: Yo, man that's going back.
I think...yeah, it was actually that train
With my mother.
There was this guy in there.
Weird as fuck, talking about
Getting ready for a boxing match.
And I asked him to teach me
Because I had gloves, too.

BOY: Teach me.

EDGAR: What?

BOY: To box. Teach me.

EDGAR: Okay.
Come here.

(The BOY *goes to* EDGAR *and takes a fighting stance.)*

EDGAR: Keep your knees slightly bent.
If your knees are locked, you can't push off
And punch right.

BOY: Okay.

EDGAR: Three punches.
Jab. Hook. Uppercut.
Like this.
(He demonstrates for the BOY.*)*
Lead with the two big knuckles.

BOY: What happens if I lead with the small knuckles?

EDGAR: You break your hand easier.
When someone throws a jab,
You throw an uppercut into their unguarded side.
If they throw any punch, you throw a punch.
Force them back.
If you want to knock them out
Try to get them on the chin or their jaw line.
You hit that sweet spot, and they're out.
And never show on your face that you're hurt.
If they know you're hurt, they're gonna come
swinging.

BOY: Never show pain on my face.

EDGAR: Yeah. That way nobody knows.

BOY: But I know.

EDGAR: And that's the only person who should know.

There's the basics. Hope you learned.

BOY: I see your pain.

EDGAR: What?

BOY: You want to go to the black hole don't you?

EDGAR: The fuck you talking about?

BOY: This train is going to the black hole
Where my mamá's waiting to take me to heaven.

EDGAR: What?
You're a fucking weirdo, man.

BOY: The soul train.

EDGAR: That old show?

BOY: Forget it.
Don't worry.
My mother told me
That people might get to heaven
Through a black hole.
But we have to die to do it.
Because only the soul can reach a black hole.

(Silence)

EDGAR: My mother used to say stuff like that, too.

BOY: I wonder how…

EDGAR: Yeah.
That good people who did right
Their souls didn't have the bad things
Weighing them down
And keeping them from going to heaven.
And bad souls were too weighed down.
And that hell is just the emptiness of space.

BOY: You really have taken a few too many to the head.

EDGAR: I read about that, you know.

BOY: Yeah?

EDGAR: Yeah on my phone.

BOY: Tell me the black hole story.

EDGAR: There's some black holes.
They're different.
They—they uh, they fuck with space and time.
Sorry, I shouldn't swear around a kid.

BOY: I don't fucking care.

EDGAR: Got it.
Well, these black holes
Because space and time breaks down
You get to…
Okay. So, like…
Everything in life is like dominoes falling.
Because of the thing that happened yesterday
You gotta deal with that shit today.
Everything happens is like a chain reaction
Following the rules of space and time.

BOY: Okay.

EDGAR: But in these special black holes.
Space and time don't exist anymore.

BOY: So, there's no chain reaction.
It's random.

EDGAR: Exactly.
And some scientists think that
Someone going in
Might be able to choose the life they want.

BOY: So, you can pick the story you want for yourself.

EDGAR: Basically.
But here's where it gets weird.
If anyone watches you

Go into the black hole, they see you die.
They see you light up on fire
Or get stretched out and like destroyed.
Or some shit like that.
But from your point of view
You're not getting destroyed.
You're choosing your future.
Like…you're going to heaven.
That's like death, right?
Everyone's scared of it and shit.
But what if everyone sees something scary
And the truth is, it's a person finally…
Finally getting the heaven they want.

BOY: What would you want
If you could get to choose the life you want??

EDGAR: I'd win my fight.

BOY: Bullshit.

EDGAR: You got a fresh mouth, kid.

BOY: Tell me the truth.

(Long silence)

EDGAR: If I could chose anything?
I'd make it to where
Our mom didn't die.
And my buddy Armando won the world title.

BOY: You wouldn't be you anymore.

EDGAR: I don't think I ever wanted to be me.

BOY: No?

EDGAR: No.

BOY: You're about to become world champion.

EDGAR: And what?
I get a visa and stay.

I do what my mother asked.
But she's still dead, and I'm still here.
Nah. I'd go back and jump out that train car with her.

(Silence)

BOY: I gotta go now.

EDGAR: I know.
It was fun.
Be good.

BOY: You did really well in your fight.
Congratulations.

EDGAR: Wait, what?

(The train stops. The compartment door flings open. Two COYOTES *[actors who play* MANUEL *and* REFEREE*] step in.)*

COYOTE 1: Nobody in here.

COYOTE 2: Fuck.

BOY: I'm here.

(The two COYOTES *notice the* BOY.*)*

COYOTE 2: It's a fucking kid.

COYOTE 1: Where's everyone else?

BOY: Gone.

COYOTE 2: Goddamn it.

COYOTE 1: You got your money?

COYOTE 2: He's a kid.
He don't got shit.

COYOTE 1: Well what the fuck we do with him?

COYOTE 2: How old are you?

BOY: Eight.

COYOTE 2: They didn't catch you, eh?

BOY: No.

COYOTE 1: You box?

BOY: No.

COYOTE 1: Why you got them gloves, then?

COYOTE 2: C'mon, leave him alone.

COYOTE 1: No, we gotta know.
Because it's one of three things.
Either he's a liar and he's a boxer
Or he's a phony trying to pretend.

COYOTE 2: He's a kid.

(COYOTE 1 *kneels down to the* BOY's *level and makes eye contact.*)

COYOTE 1: Take your best shot.

BOY: I don't want to
I don't box.
My mamá gave me these gloves.
I don't know why…

COYOTE 1: Well then, if that's the case
Your momma was a stupid bitch
Who don't know shit.

(*The* BOY *lands a hook on* COYOTE 1's *chin.* COYOTE 1 *loses consciousness.*)

COYOTE 2: Oh my God…
(*He goes to examine his partner.*)
You knocked him out.

BOY: He shouldn't have said anything about my mother.

COYOTE 2: No…you're right.
What's your name?

BOY: What's it matter?

COYOTE 2: Because what the fuck am I gonna call you?

(Silence)

BOY: Edgar Bolaños

COYOTE 2: I think we found a way for you to pay your debt.

BOY: How?

COYOTE 2: Come with me.
You ever eat a cheeseburger?

BOY: Yeah.

(COYOTE 1 *stirs and slowly stands up.*)

COYOTE 2: Get up, fucking dumbass.
We getting the champ here a burger.

COYOTE 1: *(Dazed and rubbing his chin)* Fuck...

COYOTE 2: Welcome to America, kid.
This way.

(The three of them exit. EDGAR sits in awe. ARMANDO enters.)

ARMANDO: Well, he didn't vacate the title.
And Manuel isn't pressing charges.
So, I'll be able to stay in your corner.
Fucking hell, man.
I was telling you not to fall for those tricks.
And here my dumbass...

EDGAR: It's okay.

ARMANDO: Good job making weight.

EDGAR: Thanks.

ARMANDO: You deserved to win.
Against me, you earned that win.

EDGAR: But did you throw the fight?

ARMANDO: You deserved to win the fight.

EDGAR: Why'd you do it?

ARMANDO: Because you're extraordinary
And I believe you're getting that title tonight.

Round 11

(A boxing ring. A single spotlight on the REFEREE *holding the microphone.)*

REFEREE: And now.
The main event.
Twelve rounds of boxing.
For the *(Weight class)* title of the world.
But more, much more.
A battle of pride between two top fighters.
A battle for two American dreams.
Combined between the two:
37 victories. 35 knockouts. No losses.
37 hopes dashed, and 37 dreams deferred.
To reach this stage.
To reach one final crossroads.
To the audience in attendance.
And to boxing fans all over the world.
Are you ready?

(The audience cheers.)

REFEREE: And now.
Making his way into the ring
Fighting out of Queens, New York
After an astonishing campaign
Ten fights in one year.
Nine knockouts.
A meteoric rise to the top of the ranks.
A Cinderella story for the ages.
The mandatory challenger
Seeking the title

To earn his stay in his adopted country
The United States of America
The Undocumented, The Undefeated, The Underdog
Edgar "The Extraordinary EB-1" Bolaños!!!

*(The crowd cheers. Something like Vicente Fernandez's El
Rey begins playing. The crowd cheers even louder and begins
singing along, welcoming EDGAR into his final bout. EDGAR
enters alone, fear masked behind a determined face. After he
enters the ring he holds up his glove and showboats a little.
Soon after ARMANDO holding two pads enters. EDGAR
shows off impressive skills and moves hitting the pads. The
lights darken again. A spotlight on the REFEREE.)*

REFEREE: And now
The champion.
Undefeated in twenty-seven fights
Twenty-six victories by way of knockout.
Only one fighter stands
In front of his goal
To decide the undisputed champion of the world.
Holding a ninety-six-point-three percent knockout
percentage.
The highest in division history
And himself never knocked down or knocked out in a
fight.
The fighting pride of the Bronx, New York.
El Juicio Final, El Campeon, El Demonio de Nueva
York
Manuel Gaciiiiiiaaaaaa!!!

*(MANUEL's silhouette forms behind a white screen and
begins to dance. Something like The Village People's YMCA
begins playing. EDGAR watches MANUEL's dancing,
unnerved. ARMANDO slaps EDGAR on the shoulder.)*

ARMANDO: He fucking with you.
Don't pay attention.

Keep moving.
Warmup.
Move. Move.

(MANUEL *bursts through the screen, dressed in a cape-robe and crown combo that looks like a mix of Macho Man Randy Savage and Apollo Creed, lip syncing the song as he makes his way to the ring, the title strapped diagonally across his chest. As* MANUEL *makes his way to the ring, he removes the crown and cape-robe. A mixture of boos and cheers as* MANUEL *uses his arms to form Y-M-C-A. and plays the crowd. Unlike* EDGAR, MANUEL *seems supremely confident and at ease.* EDGAR *continues to shadowbox trying to pump himself up.* MANUEL *enters the ring still showboating and playing the crowd, title glittering across his chest. The* REFEREE *motions for the two fighters to meet in the ring. They do so.)*

REFEREE: Alright gentlemen.
Good clean fight.
You got my instructions
In the locker room.
Below here is too low for both of you.

(MANUEL *leans in and touches foreheads with* EDGAR.)

MANUEL: You learn your Spanish?

EDGAR: Fuck you.

MANUEL: Three rounds.
All you get.

REFEREE: Alright, alright.
Separate.
Save it for Round 1.
Protect yourself at all times.
God bless. Good luck.
Touch gloves.
C'mon. Touch 'em.

(EDGAR *and* MANUEL *touch gloves and go to their corners. The* REFEREE *removes* MANUEL*'s title off his chest and takes it out of the ring. The* REFEREE *returns to the middle. A bell rings and the* REFEREE *signals for the fight to start.* EDGAR *and* MANUEL *make their way to the center of the ring in their stances sizing each other up.)*

ARMANDO: Like we practiced.
Dictate the pace.
Watch the jab.
Not to the ropes.
Keep him in the middle.

(MANUEL *drops his guard and leans forward, daring to take a shot.* EDGAR *obliges.)*

ARMANDO: No!

(MANUEL *immediately counters with an uppercut to the body before* EDGAR *could load his shot.* EDGAR *falls to his knees gasping.* EDGAR *appears to be kneeling before* MANUEL.)

REFEREE: Down!

MANUEL: Round one to remind you.

REFEREE: One!
Two!
Three!

(EDGAR *makes his way up. The sound of rumbling. The lights shift. He turns to the audience and begins to speak.)*

EDGAR: He spent the rest of the round
Jabbing real lightly at my face.
I couldn't hit him…
Little taps on my face.
Like he wasn't trying.
I always believed in that idea.
That with hard work and effort,
If you were persistent

You could do anything.
You could be extraordinary.
But the way Manuel moved.
Never giving me an opening.
Hitting me at will.
Laughing at every training camp.
Laughing at all my effort.
Reminding me.
Fucking reminding me.
He's extraordinary.
And me...?

(A bell rings.)

EDGAR: When the round ended
And I went back to the corner.
Armando, he was yelling something.
Giving me instructions.
Really good ones
That wasn't processing
In my head.
And as the second round began...

(A bell rings. MANUEL *resumes attacking* EDGAR. *Each line a punch.)*

MANUEL: Mi nombre.
¿Cuál es mi nombre?
Contéstame coño.
Aprende tu español.
Te enseñaré los números.
Uno. Dos. Tres.
Cuatro Cinco. Seis.
¡Ah!
¡Estás aprendiendo!

(A bell rings. MANUEL *walks to a corner.)*

EDGAR: And as the second round ended.

The ref said if I didn't throw punches
The fight was gonna be waved off.
Armando kept giving me instructions
I knew I wouldn't follow.
A bell rings again.
No.
I am not extraordinary.
I am not special.
I'm just another brown fuck
Taking a chance.
When there was never a chance in hell.
(Silence)
I only wanted to stay home…
Not…like this. Fuck…
It don't go down this way.
Not like this. Not to him. Not this piece of…
Make it to Round 4.
No. Knock him out.
Fucking all I got.
Fuck him. Fuck him. Fuck. Him.
FUCK YOU!

*(*EDGAR *lobs a similar haymaker to* ARMANDO *when he attacked* MANUEL. *It connects right to* MANUEL's *jaw.* MANUEL *falls. The rumbing stops and the lights return to normal.)*

REFEREE: Down!

ARMANDO: Yes!!
Asi, Edgar!

*(*EDGAR *raises an arm in triumph.* MANUEL *rises.* EDGAR's *hand lowers. Everything* EDGAR *had was in that punch.)*

MANUEL: You motherfuck…

*(*MANUEL *rushes right at* EDGAR. *They begin trading blows in the middle of the ring. The audience is cheering.)*

ARMANDO: Get on your bike!

Monte ese bicicleta

Keep him back with the jab.

(EDGAR *pushes off with a jab to* MANUEL'*s glove and retreats back.* MANUEL *follows but* EDGAR *keeps him at bay with the jab. A bell rings.* EDGAR *goes back to his corner.)*

ARMANDO: Good. Good.

You won that round.

Breathe. Okay.

We gotta find the knockout.

But you can't go all out in the middle.

And you gotta stop taking hits to the head.

That's how you get a brain bleed.

EDGAR: I can do it, I can do it.

ARMANDO: He ain't walking into that haymaker again.

You need to counter him.

Stay on that bike.

He gonna wanna knock you out now.

(A bell rings. EDGAR *advances on* MANUEL. *They begin trading immediately.* MANUEL *grapples with* EDGAR *and they go wrestling into the ropes.* EDGAR *uppercuts into* MANUEL'*s solar plexus.* MANUEL *sags to one knee.)*

REFEREE: Down!

(The crowd erupts as MANUEL *stands up and gets a standing eight count.* MANUEL *tries to walk down* EDGAR *but fails.* EDGAR *keeps* MANUEL *back with his jab. The bell rings.* EDGAR *makes his way back to the corner. The rumbling sound hits and the lights shift.* EDGAR *looks disoriented as he sits in his corner.)*

ARMANDO: This guy I know

He been keeping an eye.

You're up on two scorecards

The other is tied.

That motherfucker gonna chase you.
Stick behind the jab.
Clinch if he gets close.
Three minutes and you stay home.
Tres minutos.
That's all that's left.

Round 12

(*A bell rings.* EDGAR *and* MANUEL *make their way to the center. They embrace.*)

MANUEL: Feel good?
Keeping that dream alive
For just a little longer?

EDGAR: You're gonna lose.

MANUEL: Don't blink.

(*The* REFEREE *separates them. They assume their stances and the round begins.* MANUEL *immediately advances while* EDGAR *tries to hit* MANUEL *with a jab.* MANUEL *walks right through it and lands a hook right into* EDGAR's *side.* EDGAR *crashes into the ropes.*)

MANUEL: Come on.
Come here.

(MANUEL *advances,* EDGAR *tries to get away.* MANUEL *cuts the ring off and corners* EDGAR *who tries to clinch but* MANUEL *unloads on* EDGAR's *abdomen.*)

MANUEL: You're here because
I let you stay here.

(EDGAR *falls. The* REFEREE *gets in the way.*)

REFEREE: Down!

(MANUEL *goes to a corner to wait.* EDGAR *struggles to get as the rumbling grows louder.*)

MANUEL: It felt good, right?
Thinking you could win.
It was a beautiful dream.
You thought you were special.
Now you see.
You ain't shit.

(EDGAR *has stood up. The* BOY *enters.*)

REFEREE: Are you okay?

(EDGAR *stares in confusion at the* BOY. *The* REFEREE *and*
MANUEL *exit.* EDGAR *goes to the bassinet and looks at the*
BOY, *still bewildered.*)

EDGAR: What?

BOY: You got hit hard, didn't you?
You can't hear anything.
Don't worry, she's coming.

(*The* MAMÁ *enters.* EDGAR *sees her and almost loses it.*)

MAMÁ: Edgar…I need you to listen to me.

EDGAR: Mamá…

MAMÁ: You did really good.

EDGAR: Mamá, I'm scared.

MAMÁ: I know. I know.
Mijo, I know.

EDGAR: Please don't go again.
I need you.

MAMÁ: I need you too.
I need you to live.
I need you to keep going.
Everything you got, do you understand?
Bring that belt home.

EDGAR: I can't.

MAMÁ: You can do anything.

EDGAR: That's a lie Mamá.
I'm gonna fail.
Without you, I'm gonna…

MAMÁ: Listen now.
You are fucking extraordinary.
Do you understand me?

EDGAR: Mamá, please.

MAMÁ: Make your own legacy.
With your fists.
With your two hands.
Do better. Be better. You are better.
One day you'll understand.

(The MAMÁ *and* BOY *exit. The* REFEREE *re-enters with* MANUEL. *The* REFEREE *stands in front of* EDGAR.*)*

REFEREE: Are you okay?
Can you go on?

*(*EDGAR *nods. The* REFEREE *looks over* EDGAR *and allows the fight to continue.)*

MANUEL: There you go.
To the end.
I like that.

EDGAR: To the end. Goddamn right.

*(*EDGAR *and* MANUEL *meet in the middle and begin trading blows.* MANUEL *takes a blow to the face and* EDGAR *to the body from* MANUEL's *counter. They back off.* EDGAR's *arms fall to his sides. They stare at each other.* EDGAR *smiles.)*

EDGAR: I can't lift up my arms.

*(*EDGAR *and* MANUEL *laugh.)*

MANUEL: Eleven fights in a year
Will do that to you.

EDGAR: Fuck me, right?

(He laughs again, hollow.)

MANUEL: That's some shit.

Time to wake up.

Dream's over.

Sorry EB-1.

(EDGAR forces his hands up. MANUEL advances toward EDGAR. Blackout. A bell rings.)

Round 13

(Stage completely dark except for the spotlight on EDGAR wrapped with a boxing world title diagonally across his chest, in that way that the WBC title hangs on a boxer after a victory. In front of him, a scale.)

EDGAR: I started boxing when I was eight.

I was wearing some boxing gloves my mother gave me before she died. And some guy, right?

He was fucking with me. Made fun of me and tried getting me angry. He asked me to punch him in the face.

And I didn't want to fight.

Fucking truth be told, I don't like to fight.

I don't like hitting people, I don't like getting hit.

But when that fucker said shit about my mother.

That's all it took. I took the lessons I taught myself and knocked him the fuck out.

He had a buddy there with him and he took me to a gym.

I became a boxer.

I became a money maker.

I won fights.

I threw fights.

They made cash.

I got to live another day

In the country my mother died to get into.
That was twenty years ago.
And when I tried walking away from the ring,
I got me a message telling me that my sports visa
The one those men got for me to make sure I could fight
Was going to expire.
No chance of renewal.
I got a year before I get my ass deported.
Unless…I put them gloves back on and proved I was extraordinary enough to be worthy to stay.
That's the thing, right? Set up the story with some bad shit that I gotta overcome to prove I belong in the place I called home for twenty years. That's that shit they hold over you, right? The people that don't gotta prove themselves like to make everyone else do a fucking song and dance to prove, to fucking prove that you deserve to live where you live.
I got a theory, right? Those people who say that they wouldn't change a single thing if they had a chance are lying motherfuckers who're trying to trick themselves into thinking the shit they went through was necessary. But I ain't lying to myself.
I'd change it all.
The greatest mistakes of my life was letting my mother go and taking a swing at a motherfucker who spit on her memory.
I'd change those two things. If I could get a wish. I'd give back the belt. I'd give back every single fucking thing I earned. I'd wish the last twenty years away. Because after they took my mother away, the last twenty years didn't mean shit.
Because I shit you not, becoming a champion ain't shit when your mother ain't here to celebrate it. Being able

to stay home ain't shit when you got no family waiting at home.

Life ain't worth it. Life's not worth it when a child's separated from his mother.

I'd wish I hugged her a little longer. I'd wish I jumped out with her and died there. I wish we'd died together on the soul train going to God's country where the only thing that's needed is a soul that's good, and you don't have to hurt others to get your chance to be a citizen.

(Silence)

But that's not the ending I get, is it?

No.

No, instead I hit Manuel with that sweet left hook right to the chin. He crumbles. The ref waves it off.

And the new...!

I did it. I proved it. I'm extraordinary.

So? Now what? The visa. And then?

And then?

(The REFEREE *enters holding a mic. A rumbling as a black hole opens behind them.)*

REFEREE: Congratulations, Edgar
On becoming the new world champion.

EDGAR: World champion...

REFEREE: Yes. You must be in shock.
A stunning left hook to the chin.
Take us through the fight.

EDGAR: Extraordinary...

(EDGAR looks behind himself and sees the black hole. He smiles.)

EDGAR: Goddamn...

(The sound of a train)

EDGAR: It's beautiful...

REFEREE: I'm sorry, what?

(EDGAR *throws the world champion's belt to the ground. He vomits and falls to the ground, convulsing.* ARMANDO *enters and sees* EDGAR *falling. He rushes to* EDGAR *and pushes past the* REFEREE.)

ARMANDO: Get the fuck out of my way.
Move. Move. That's my fighter.
Champ—champion.
How you doing?
No, no, no.
Get up. Come on now.

EDGAR: I'm not…I'm not gonna…

ARMANDO: You're not going on me now.
You just won the belt, mijo.

EDGAR: *(Groggy incoherent)*
I'm the one…go on the soul train.

ARMANDO: That's right, that's right.
Whatever you say, Eddie.
No, don't, don't fall asleep…

(*The black hole roars, changing the universe. The lights shift.* ARMANDO *is stunned as* EDGAR *stands. He takes off* ARMANDO's *clothes until he is down to boxing trunks.* EDGAR *picks up the world title and wraps it around* ARMANDO's *chest. He hugs* ARMANDO, *who doesn't understand what's happening.*)

EDGAR: Payment.
For services rendered.

ARMANDO: What?

(EDGAR *exits. The lights shift back, the black hole still open and the* REFEREE *comes to* ARMANDO.)

REFEREE: Congratulations to you Armando
For pulling off the upset in Round 1

Against Manuel Garcia and claiming the title.
A dream fulfilled, right?

*(*ARMANDO *stares blankly at the* REFEREE.*)*

REFEREE: You deserve it.

(Silence. ARMANDO *takes the belt off and holds it close, trying to fight back tears.)*

Round 14

(Freight train compartment rattling. The MAMÁ *and* BOY *returned to the scene before the* MAMÁ *sacrifices herself.)*

MAMÁ: You need to go hide now.

BOY: I don't want to.

MAMÁ: Please...

(The BOY *senses what's to come. He takes off his gloves and hugs the* MAMÁ *, fingers wrapping around her clothes. The yelling increases in volume and rattling from the compartment doors grows more violent. She pulls him off and levels her gaze at him.)*

MAMÁ: To answer your question...
Every moment. Every heartbeat
From your first breath to my last gasp.
This very moment.
Worth it.
You're worth it.

BOY: Why?

MAMÁ: Because you're extraordinary.

(The BOY *holds fast to the* MAMÁ *refusing to let go.)*

BOY: I'm not letting go.

MAMÁ: Edgar, please go hide.

BOY: No.

(EDGAR *enters and holds the door before it can be opened. A crash. The door stops rattling.*)

VOICE: *(Outside)*
Déjalo, cabrón.
No hay nadie ahí.
Venga, venga.

(*The sounds of footsteps fading. Silence. After a moment, the train begins moving.*)

MAMÁ: Oh my God…

(*The* BOY *watches* EDGAR *as he fades away. They wave at each other. The black hole closes. The* BOY *holds onto his mother and she onto him, both on the train to God's country, or the US, whichever comes first. The lights fade. The sound of the train shifts to the sound of a holter monitor as it flatlines.*)

Round 15

(*The sound of flatlining fades. Dim lights rise on the ring. In the middle of the ring is the world title, a water bottle, the gun, and a pair of boxing gloves. The black hole opens and pulls in the light causing a blackout. Sound of a boxing bell. Silence.*)

END OF PLAY

www.ingramcontent.com/pod-product-compliance
Lightning Source LLC
Chambersburg PA
CBHW052210090426
42741CB00010B/2481